T0062927

Share My Soul

"A gift to the world."

Yosipa

BALBOA
PRESS

A DIVISION OF HAY HOUSE

Balboa Press books may be ordered through booksellers or by contacting:

Balboa Press
A Division of Hay House
1663 Liberty Drive
Bloomington, IN 47403
www.balboapress.com.au
1-(877) 407-4847

ISBN: 978-1-4525-0973-0 (sc)
ISBN: 978-1-4525-0974-7 (e)

Because of the dynamic nature of the Internet, any web addresses or links contained in this book may have changed since publication and may no longer be valid. The views expressed in this work are solely those of the author and do not necessarily reflect the views of the publisher, and the publisher hereby disclaims any responsibility for them.

The author of this book does not dispense medical advice or prescribe the use of any technique as a form of treatment for physical, emotional, or medical problems without the advice of a physician, either directly or indirectly. The intent of the author is only to offer information of a general nature to help you in your quest for emotional and spiritual well-being. In the event you use any of the information in this book for yourself, which is your constitutional right, the author and the publisher assume no responsibility for your actions.

Any people depicted in stock imagery provided by Thinkstock are models, and such images are being used for illustrative purposes only.
Certain stock imagery © Thinkstock.

Printed in the United States of America

Balboa Press rev. date: 04/05/2013

Dedicated to experience—
for that is how we learn!
Also to my three beautiful, beloved daughters,
Sophia, Tahlia, and Ella.

The first poem that I wrote was "Call Of The Wild" about twenty years ago in Paddington, Sydney. That poem is more relevant to today. I was inspired to write from all the experiences I gathered when I moved to Byron Bay in 1996, where I met lifelong friends and basically spent my time trying to figure out what life was about. I had a yearning to understand life in all its shades. At the turn of the century, this style of poetry started to emerge from within, and I wanted to share it with humanity, so this is how the book came to be.

One of my favourite quotes was found on a Baci chocolate wrapper and it has always resonated with me:

> Words are eternal: when speaking them
> or writing them, be aware of their eternity.
> —Anonymous

Yosipa

Table of Contents

Call Of The Wild 1

My Muse 4

Endless Pink Roses 5

Eclipse 6

Only You 7

Colours 8

Untamed 9

Curtains Of Clouds 10

True Love 11

Heart-Strings 12

My Thousand Pieces 13

Your Own Beauty 14

Sense Of Flow 15

Faded Memories 16

Garden Of Gardens 17

Surfer 18

Fragrance 19

Heartbreak 20

The Desert 21

Forever 22

Unrequited Love 23

Love Is My Song 24

Passion 25

Treasure 26

My Childhood 27

Purity 28

Desert Diamonds 29

Mysterious Entity 30
Friends 31
One 32
Set Yourself Free 33
Bleeding Through Tears 34
Be Simple 35
A Hidden Language 36
Whispering Gratitude 37
Ghost Of An Angel 38
Snow And Jasmine 39
Why? 40
Believe 41
My Daughters 42
Kiss The Sky 43
A Passionate Plea 44
Poet's Soul 45
Pearls 46
Whispers 47
Try 48
Silent 49
Celine 50
Eternity 51
Timing 52
A Dream 53

Call Of The Wild

In mankind's evolution,
we neglected our Mother Earth,
creating so much pollution,
she is waiting for a rebirth.

The call of her children
comes from the wilderness,
a roar from a lion's den
to clean up our mess.

What happened to simplicity,
When people lived off the land?
Now we have concrete jungles in the city
built from mankind's hands.

Humanity is struggling to survive
in the world that we created.
Nature gave us bees and a hive,
and we gave back toxic lead.

We pay money for nature's life—
fruits, vegetables, and grains,
innocent animals that face the knife.
Tell me, where are the gains?

Some lifestyles became robotic
and no longer feel feelings,
causing their bodies to become sick
from all the wheeling and dealing.

Who created money?
Mother Earth didn't; she created beauty
that's as sweet as honey.
To heal the Earth is our duty.

Why are we killing our brothers
for money that is only paper?
To value yourself and others
is something that does matter.

What happens in the end
if we don't stop this now?
This is not some passing trend,
when you kill the last cow.

We are all in this together.
Can we learn to accept,
Extending our love to each other
and welcome the annoying insect?

What do we have remaining,
when all the wildlife is gone
and the world is no longer standing?
We roam this path alone.

We have taken nature for granted,
for she is our home,
trees that were planted,
and seeds that were sown.

The Earth is our home.
She gave us all the tools,
yet we created foam
for our survival; can we stop being fools?

We were born without possessions.
All we wanted was love,
and part of that creation
was a pure white dove.

My Muse

My muse,
inspired
by my dream
for passion
of the one,
the only one
who would complete me,
instead reflected
my completeness
after being shattered
to a thousand pieces.

Endless Pink Roses

Once,
my being unfolded,
endless pink roses,
the witness in me
sat back
and engulfed
the perfume.

Eclipse

I will be the moon,
you will be the sun;
once in a while,
we'll come together
as an eclipse
and explode
amongst the stars.

Only You

Breathe fire
from the depths
of your cauldron.
Manifest the creations,
born to you—
only you!

Colours

Happily die
to the cocoon
that binds your wings,
beautiful butterfly,
and show the world
your colours.

Untamed

Wild,
untamed heart,
running,
afraid of itself.
What a shame
to run from
the very beauty
you are seeking.

Curtains Of Clouds

The curtains of clouds
have disappeared,
so the stars
may have the stage
yet again.

True Love

Everyone gets
to experience true love
inside the temple
of one's
own being.

Heart-Strings

I asked once,
"Where are you?"
You were right here,
pulling at my heartstrings,
untying each one
so that I may fly.

My Thousand Pieces

Outside I act the queen.
Inside,
I'm a golden child.
Outside you act the chameleon.
Inside,
you are your own king.
Because of you,
my thousand pieces of me
became one.

Your Own Beauty

If you were
free in yourself,
you wouldn't be so
afraid to love,
to be intimate,
looking into another
love's eyes
and maybe for
the first time,
seeing your own
beauty.

Sense Of Flow

Colours parade
in a stream of dance,
moving into
a sea of energy.
Leaving a sense of flow,
it gives me
wings to fly
out of my body,
into my soul.

Faded Memories

Distant lands appear now,
gondolas, spring, and cherry wine,
faded memories
of a lost time,
a love that was never
meant to be.

Garden Of Gardens

Answer
never-ending questions
with love.
Mystery awaits
at every turn,
uprooting any ideals
that may still remain
in the garden of gardens.

Surfer

A surfer
is one with
the ocean
that's his stage.
Riding to her motion,
he feels free
from the cage.

Fragrance

Flowers
grow beneath
what is seen.
What is not seen,
fragrance,
invisible,
so sweet.

Heartbreak

Young heart, old soul,
guide me
to higher ground.
Why was I so
forgiving
to a dream?

The Desert

Desert butterfly,
blown by the
wind,
where to go
in this endless
sanctuary?

Forever

I didn't know
the meaning
of forever
until I wanted

it.

Unrequited Love

I've known you before,
other times,
different lands.
You're familiar but different
this time,
treading the depths of
darkness
in ourselves,
in each other.
Is it unrequited love
from long ago?

Love Is My Song

Love is written in the stars,
love is magic like the moon,
love is as deep as the ocean,
love is when you feel your heart flutter,
love is when you melt like butter,
love is the sparkle in one's eyes,
love is my dream
and all the good things in between—
love is my song.

Passion

Passion is a fire
burning inside,
waiting to dance
with another flame.

Treasure

Golden threads
link us to infinity.
Where?
Inside of us,
dive in and go deep.
Do not be afraid,
as it is only treasure
you will find.

My Childhood

No more pain, little girl,
come out and play.
There's a whole world
waiting,
no more hiding,
the sun is shining.

Purity

Everything,
a breath away, so close,
see without your eyes
but with your knowing,
listen without the ears
but with your intuition,
smell without the nose
but with your being,
taste without the tongue
but with your soul,
touch without the hands
but with your Spirit.
What is left?
Nothing but purity.

Desert Diamonds

In the vastness,
underneath diamonds,
my eyes are
on fire.
Ruby red warms us.

Mysterious Entity

Everything passes and fades,

the euphoria of togetherness

dies eventually,

left alone,

until that void inside

is filled

once again

with another yearning,

a mysterious entity

I have come to

accept.

Friends

Here's where the story ends
and laughter begins,
when we all came together
to find ourselves.
We laughed,
we cried,
and never lost the
spirit of life.
We faced the past
to enjoy the present
and only imagine what
our future could be.

One

Many mirrors,

many illusions,

break

to remember

one love,

one truth,

one . . .

Set Yourself Free

Talk to me,
tell me what's locked up
inside your walls.
I already know,
but you need a voice
to free yourself from the past
which keeps you bound
to the now.

Cry, dear heart.
Let sorrows wash away
past's that no longer
serve the present.
Give the gift to yourself,
set yourself free.

The battle is inside,
but the beauty
is worth it
when you see
your own smile.

Bleeding Through Tears

Bleeding through tears,

my heart aches,

birth of love is present,

pain.

Does it ever stop?

Momentarily,

in the depths of a

light-filled time.

Be Simple

Rhythm of a song
moved me into another land.
Sun rays caress the clouds,
the ocean kisses the shore,
leaves shake the tree,
rocks absorb nothing,
nothing is everything.
Stay wilder than the wind
for a taste of freedom,
yours and mine.
Be simple,
dance in the stars,
and wish me well
until we meet again my friend.

A Hidden Language

Poetry,

a hidden language,

feel between the lines,

beyond the words,

is a key.

Whispering Gratitude

Magic is mystery
for you
and a cure for me,
whispering gratitude.

Ghost Of An Angel

My love,
his face I longed for.
Your energy
walked before yourself.
I felt the ghost
of an angel.

Snow And Jasmine

The soul of a poet,
suppressed amongst chaos,
a garden I carry,
white and fragrant,
like snow and jasmine
combined.

Why?

After so many centuries,
multiple lifetimes,
and ancient histories,
people still don't know
how to love each other.
Why?

Believe

I cannot give you
what you think you want;
you are everything already
and more.
It's
all inside of you.
Believe.

My Daughters

Rainbow chalk,
washed away by the rain,
colours in the driveway,
afternoon child's play.

Kiss The Sky

Who knows where her destiny lies?
I know she likes
dancing with butterflies.
The moment never ends
as she calls them her friends,
watching them float on by.
Sophia, too, will one day
kiss the sky.

A Passionate Plea

I'm looking in your eyes
for some mystery,
between love,
a passionate plea to the world,
is my destiny.

Poet's Soul

Bursts of words,
pen on paper,
flowing mind,
writing a book that only I may read.
Who cares enough to print
a poet's soul?

Pearls

Through honesty about
imperfections,
we become perfect.
Like pearls of
wisdom.

Whispers

The voice inside,
friend or foe?
Your guide to life,
follow the whispers
from heaven.

Try

Life will make you
get up and try,
push you, test you
and own you,
so you become
who you are meant to be.

Silent

Your inner voice
gets louder,
as the rush of the world
becomes silent.

Celine

A language, French.
Music to my ears,
Celine,
your voice softens
the world.
Je taime.

Eternity

Life,
fragile,
cradle each other,
before you know it,
eternity calls.

Timing

Endless possibilities,
when the fear resides.
It's all in the timing
of what will be,
shall be.

A Dream

One lives through
many experiences—
suffering, pain, anger, confusion,
love, hope, joy, and laughter—
only to remember
it was all a dream.
Let's make it a great ONE!